THE CLASSROOM

Maya stared down at her half-eaten sandwich, the crusts stubbornly refusing to disappear.

Lunchtime in Room 3B was usually a symphony of chatter and clattering lunchboxes, but today, the sounds seemed to grate on her ears.

Maya was... different. At least, that's what people seemed to think.

She loved numbers and could solve complex equations in her head, but sometimes struggled to understand simple jokes.

She could talk for hours about the migration patterns of monarch butterflies, but often found herself speechless when someone asked a casual question like, "How's it going?"

How's it going?

Her hands were always in motion, fiddling with her hair, tapping her fingers, or bouncing her leg. And kids, well, kids could be... unkind.

Then there was Alex. Alex was also... different. Alex had an Educational Assistant, Sarah, who was always beside him.

Alex often yelled, loud, piercing shouts that made Maya jump. He sometimes threw things when he got upset, and once, just last week, he'd had a full-blown meltdown.

Books had been flung, chairs had been overturned, and the entire class had to be evacuated to the library while Sarah tried to calm him down.

Afterward, Maya had heard the whispers. "Why is he so disruptive." "Why is he even in our class?" "It's not fair to the rest of us."

She understood the frustration. Alex's outbursts made it hard to concentrate. But she also saw the flicker of fear in his eyes sometimes, a lost and confused look that mirrored her own.

"He's got autism," she'd overheard a few kids saying. "That's why he acts like that." The word "autism" hung in the air, heavy and undefined.

That evening, Maya sat at the kitchen table, pushing peas around her plate. Her mom, noticing her frown, sat down beside her. "Rough day, sweetie?"

"They were talking about Alex again. Saying he's disruptive because he has autism." Her mom sighed gently. "People don't always understand, Maya."

"I know," Maya mumbled. "But... they think that's all autism is. Yelling and throwing things. And... what if they think I'm like...Alex?"

Her mom wrapped an arm around her. "Oh, honey. I understand your worry. But autism isn't one thing—it's a spectrum of many things. Everyone's brain has its own design."

"Some people have more challenges with sounds. Others might struggle with talking, or need things to stay the same. But no two people are the same."

Her mom smiled. "You can think of it like a colour wheel. Each section is a trait, like social skills, anxiety, or coordination. Everyone has a different place on the wheel."

The next day, Mrs. Davis announced a class project on understanding how people think and feel in different ways. Maya's stomach fluttered. Was this her moment?

Mrs. Davis smiled at the class. "Our brains are like colourful wheels—each with different strengths and needs. That's how we understand autism."

Autism is a mosaic, Not a Level

"People used to think autism was like a straight line," Mrs. Davis said, drawing one on the board. "But that line only says more or less, and that's not right. Because..." She turned to the color wheel. "Autism isn't more or less—it's a spectrum. Like this!" "Each person has their own mix of colors. Some bright, some soft, some in between. That's what makes each person's brain special."

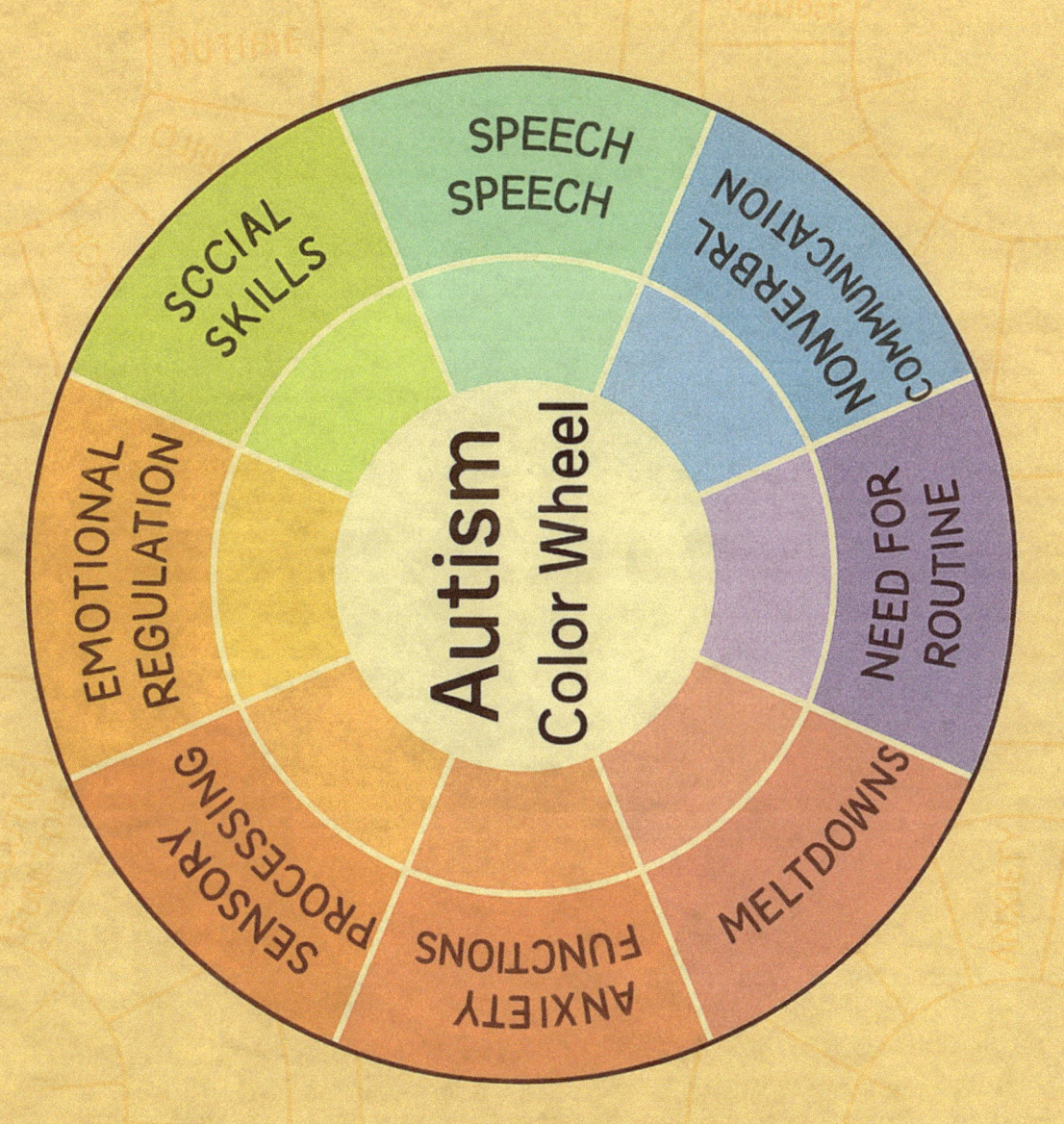

She pointed to a poster of the Autism Colour Wheel. "See? Some people may struggle with speech. Others may need routines. Everyone's wheel is unique."

Then, Mrs. Davis gave Maya an encouraging nod. They had talked about this moment earlier. "Maya has something she would like to share with you all," she said gently. Maya's heart leaped into her throat–but she nodded.

Autism is a mosaic, not a level.

"I... I'm autistic," Maya said. She paused, then added, "Autism can look different in each person. This is just how it looks for me."

The title on the board read: "Our Minds Are Made of Many Colours."
Maya smiled as Alex built a tower with Sarah beside him. It felt like something new had begun.

My Unique Mind Wheel

Every brain is different—and that's a beautiful thing! Use the color wheel below to reflect on your own strengths and challenges. Color in each section to show how much it feels like "you" right now. Remember: no two wheels will ever look the same.

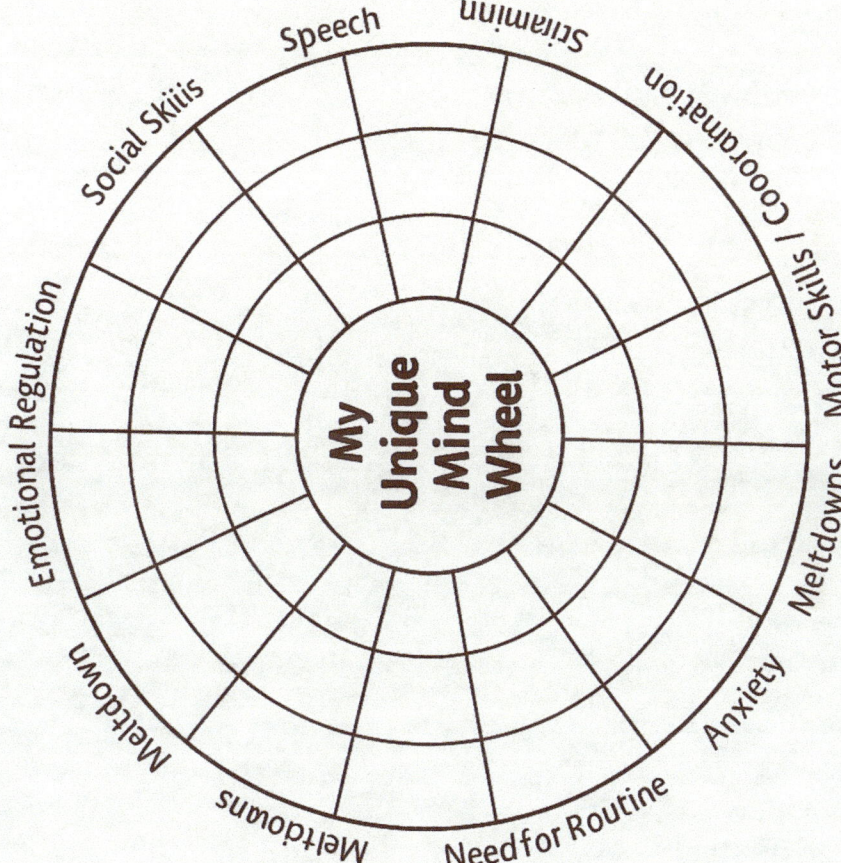

Wheel sections: Speech, Stimming, Coordination, Motor Skills / Coordination, Meltdowns, Anxiety, Need for Routine, Meltdowns, Meltdown, Emotional Regulation, Social Skills

Something i wish others understood about me is… _____